9/14

GHOST SHIPS

by Adrienne Montgomerie

Crabtree Publishing Company
www.crabtreebooks.com

Crabtree Publishing Company

www.crabtreebooks.com

Author: Adrienne Montgomerie
Project Coordinator: Kathy Middleton
Editors: Molly Aloian, Tim Cooke
Proofreader: Reagan Miller
Designer: Lynne Lennon
Cover Design: Margaret Amy Salter
Picture Researcher: Andrew Webb
Picture Manager: Sophie Mortimer
Art Director: Jeni Child
Editorial Director: Lindsey Lowe
Children's Publisher: Anne O'Daly
**Production Coordinator and
    Prepress Technician:** Margaret Amy Salter
Print Coordinator: Katherine Berti

Photographs
Cover: Shutterstock: AdamEdwards
Interior: Alamy: dieKleinert 10, Zach Holmes 21, Kevin Schafer 12; **Bridgeman Art Library:** Christie's Images/Private Collection 15, Russell-Cotes Art Gallery 14–15; **Corbis:** Bettmann 19, 20; **Library of Congress:** 23; **Mary Evans Picture Library:** 9; **Shutterstock:** 6, 8, 22, Yana Gayvoronskaya 5, Chris Geszvain 29, Rivendell Digital Studio 28, Bruce Rolf 16, Alfredo Schaufelberger 13, Wild Arctic Pictures 17; **Thinkstock:** Dorling Kinderslay 3–5, Hemera 7, istockphoto 18, LifeSize 26, Top Photo Group 27; **Topfoto:** 24, The Granger Collection 11, Topham Picturepoint 25.

Library and Archives Canada Cataloguing in Publication

Montgomerie, Adrienne
    Ghost ships / Adrienne Montgomerie.

(Mystery files)
Includes index.
Issued also in electronic formats.
ISBN 978-0-7787-8008-3 (bound).--ISBN 978-0-7787-8013-7 (pbk.)

    1. Shipwrecks--Juvenile literature. 2. Marine accidents--Juvenile literature. I. Title. II. Series: Mystery files (St. Catharines, Ont.)

G525.M66 2012   j910.4'52   C2012-906830-6

Library of Congress Cataloging-in-Publication Data

CIP available at Library of Congress

Crabtree Publishing Company
www.crabtreebooks.com   1-800-387-7650

Published in Canada
Crabtree Publishing
616 Welland Ave.
St. Catharines, ON
L2M 5V6

Published in the United States
Crabtree Publishing
PMB 59051
350 Fifth Avenue, 59th Floor
New York, New York 10118

Published by CRABTREE PUBLISHING COMPANY in 2013
Copyright © 2013 Brown Bear Books Ltd

Contents

Introduction

Oceans cover nearly three-quarters of the Earth's surface—and many people believe them to be among its most haunted places. For centuries, sailors have reported strange sightings at sea: bright lights, weird creatures such as mermaids, and ghostly ships steered by the souls of the dead. Some of these **phenomena** can be explained by natural events such as shooting stars and fog, or by the imaginations of sailors alone in the middle of the vast oceans. Seeing seals or walruses through mist, for example, might have led to descriptions of mermaids. But some stories seem to have no simple explanation.

Ghostly Visions

Some legends describe ghostly vessels that are doomed to sail the oceans forever, with a crew of the dead. Other ghost ships are said to be visions of real ships that were wrecked in the past. In sailors' stories, seeing such a vessel is often a sign that disaster is about to strike.

Mystery words...

phenomena: things that are not easily explained

Mysterious Realm

The sea holds many other mysteries, such as ships with crews that have vanished for no obvious reason or who have been struck dead. Many ships have gone missing completely. Did they simply sink or meet a more suspicious fate?

In this book, you will read a range of stories about the oceans, the spirits that sail them, and the sailors whose fate remains unknown.

The open seas have inspired many tales of mystery and horror.

The Flying DUTCHMAN

The Flying Dutchman is the world's most famous ghost ship. In legends, it is a Dutch man-of-war that sank in the 17th century. It is doomed to sail the oceans forever. It can never dock, because the crew are dead, so it just keeps sailing.

The ship appears in the ocean surrouded in a ghostly glowing light. Its sails are full of wind, even if the air is still. Sailors dread seeing *The Flying Dutchman*. The ship is said to be an omen, or sign, of disaster ahead.

The crew is doomed to sail forever as a punishment for a crime long ago. When *The Flying Dutchman* approaches another ship, the crew try to pass on messages to be taken to shore. The messages are for people who have been dead for centuries.

Mystery words...

man-of-war: a heavily armed warship with sails

Common Story

The Flying Dutchman has inspired many writers and artists. In 1843, the German composer Richard Wagner even wrote an opera about it, called *The Flying Dutchman*. That made the legend even more famous. More recently, the ship was featured in the *Pirates of the Caribbean* movies.

One explanation for ghost ships is that they are illusions. Strange light, mists, and clouds create reflections of real ships far away across the water. But that doesn't explain why old-fashioned sailing ships often seem to appear.

According to legends, The Flying Dutchman can never stop sailing.

The Mary CELESTE

The fate of the ship's crew is one of the great sea mysteries.

Everything seemed normal. The sea was calm. The merchant ship's sails were up and it was heading for the Strait of Gibraltar, where the Mediterranean Sea joins the Atlantic Ocean. But the ship was abandoned. There was no sign of the crew.

Mystery words...

merchant ship: a ship used to carry cargo for trade

It was December 1872 and the ship was the U.S. vessel *Mary Celeste*. What became of the ten people on board is one of the most famous of all sea mysteries. There were signs that they had abandoned ship in a hurry. They had left their valuables behind. One of the lifeboats was missing. But there was no obvious reason to leave the ship. There was no damage to suggest the ship had been caught in a storm.

The ship was under full sail when it was discovered.

Mystery File: DANGEROUS CARGO

The *Mary Celeste's* cargo was barrels of alcohol. It was the most dangerous cargo the ship had ever carried. One theory about the ship's fate is that the crew abandoned it because they thought the alcohol was about to explode. That is the latest theory about why the ship was abandoned..

Abandon Ship

One possible explanation is that the ship had been attacked by pirates. But if that was the case, why did the pirates not take anything from the ship? Perhaps the sailors were sucked off the ship by a water spout or knocked overboard by a huge wave. It's likely that we'll never know the true answer.

The Blazing
STEAMSHIP

On some dark nights, an eerie sight is said to appear on the Tombigbee River in Alabama. It is an old-fashioned paddle steamer, engulfed in flames. It sank there over 150 years ago.

The ship appears in the middle of a ball of flame.

The *Eliza Battle* caught fire and sank on the Tombigbee in 1858. Twenty-six people died in the disaster: about half the people on board.

The *Eliza Battle* was a luxurious vessel. It had a **paddle wheel** on each side, driven by a steam engine. Along with passengers, the ship carried cargo such as cotton from farms to markets. On the night of the disaster, a spark set fire to the cotton cargo, which burned easily.

Mystery words...

paddle wheel: a wheel driven by a motor to move a boat

River Wreck

The passsengers jumped into the cold water to escape. The *Eliza Battle* burned and then sank. The boat is still on the bottom of the river, only 28 feet (8.5 meters) below the surface. When the steamer appears fully aflame on the river, local people believe it is an omen, or sign, of disaster ahead.

Sparks from the steamer's engines may have started the blaze.

Many ghost ships are said to be **visions** of vessels that sank. Another example is the ghost ship *Isidore*, which was wrecked off the coast of Maine in 1842. Could these really be ghosts surfacing from the past?

11

Party of the DEAD

Chileans say that you hear the *Caleuche* before you see it. The sounds of a party can be heard from the legendary ghost ship of Chiloé Island, off the southern coast of Chile. But the *Caleuche* is no ordinary ship, and this is no ordinary party. The only guests are the souls of the dead.

The Caleuche *sails the waters around Chiloé Island.*

The *Caleuche* appears at night, but is lit up with white light. The sounds of the party fill the air. The large sails of the three masts are always full of wind. The crew of the ghost ship are said to be the souls of people who drowned, brought on board to work, or kidnapped sailors who have been dead for centuries. Their officers are said to be mermaids and warlocks. According to local myths, dead souls who are taken on board enjoy life as if they were alive again, which is why people say they can hear the sounds of a party.

More Than a Ship

In Chilean mythology, the *Caleuche* is not just a ship. It is like a living being. Like another famous ghost ship, *The Flying Dutchman*, the *Caleuche* is said to be able to sink beneath the waves and **navigate** underwater.

Mystery File:
PARTY TIME

Many peoples have myths about the dead holding parties, like the souls on the *Caleuche*. In Viking myths, for example, warriors who died bravely in battle gather in Valhalla. They enjoy endless feasting with their former companions.

Mystery words...

navigate: to work out and follow a course of direction

Ghosts of the
SANDS

The Goodwin Sands is one of the most haunted places in the oceans. For centuries, vessels in the English Channel have sunk in the shallow waters of the treacherous sandbank. The sands are haunted by the ghosts of these ships.

One of the ghostly vessels is the *Lady Lovibond*, which sank on the sands in 1748. The ship's captain, Simon Reed, had just got married. He ignored the traditional sailors' **superstition** that it was bad luck to have a woman on board. Reed took his new bride on a voyage.

The wrecks of old ships are all over the Goodwin Sands.

The ship's first mate also loved Reed's wife. In a jealous rage, he ran the ship aground. Everyone onboard drowned. Today, the ship is said to appear every 50 years, bathed in a greenish glow.

More Ghosts

Other ghost ships that haunt the sands include the SS *Montrose*, a liner from the early 20th century, and a man-of-war, the *Shrewsbury*. The area was also said to be home to an ancient island named Lomea. No trace of Lomea has ever been found. Perhaps the lost island is another ghost of the sands.

The 10-mile (16-km) sandbank was the scene of many wrecks.

Mystery File: SUPERSTITIONS

Not taking a woman onboard is one of many naval superstitions. Others include not setting sail on a Friday, not taking bananas on a fishing boat, and not cutting your hair on board. All these things are said to bring bad luck.

Mystery words...

superstition: a belief that events can magically create bad luck

Adrift in the ICE

When the ship was found, everything about *Octavius* seemed normal. The crew members were in place. The captain was sitting at his desk, writing the ship's log. But *Octavius* had been drifitng in the Arctic for 13 years and the men were frozen solid.

Octavius was found drifting off the west coast of Greenland, in the North Atlantic Ocean, in 1775. But when the sailors who found it went aboard, they saw everyone was dead. The last entry in the ship's log was dated 13 years earlier. The ship had been drifting ever since.

The ship was found drifting silently off Greenland.

The Arctic Ocean was a shortcut between Asia and Europe.

Mystery File:
JENNY'S STORY

The **schooner** *Jenny* was discovered in 1840, after 17 years stuck in ice in the Antarctic. Parts of the story of *Jenny* are identical to that of *Octavius*. Perhaps the stories were based on one another; but does that mean that neither was true?

Trapped!

Octavius was returning from East Asia to England. Its captain followed the Northwest Passage, at the top of North America. It was a risk, because the Arctic waters were frozen for much of the year.

Octavius was trapped in the ice. After the crew died, the ship moved with the ice over 1,860 miles (2,993 kilometers) before it was found. The freezing temperatures had preserved the bodies of the crew perfectly.

Mystery words...

log: the official record of a ship's voyage

Mystery Ship of the TITANIC

The sinking of the *Titanic* in 1912 is one of the most famous of all ocean disasters. The liner was on its first voyage when it struck an iceberg in the middle of the Atlantic. There were not enough lifeboats for all the people onboard. Some 1,500 people lost their lives.

Flares are visible for many miles.

Titanic hit the iceberg in the middle of the night. At once, the ship's crew began to fire **flares** and send distress signals by radio. Many ships picked up the signals and began steaming toward *Titanic*'s position. But the ship was filling up fast with water. The other ships were too far away to reach it before it sank. There was one chance, however. Survivors reported seeing another ship on the horizon.

Mystery words...

flares: bright lights fired into the sky as distress signals

Mystery Ship

The ship could easily have come to help. But it did not react to the flares or to the SOS signals. *Titanic* was left to sink.

What was the name of the mystery ship? Why didn't it help? The ship has never been identified. No other ships were reported to have been in the area. Some survivors could not even remember seeing it. Had it been a real ship? Or was it a ghost vessel, drawn toward the approaching disaster?

Many stories surround the sinking of the *Titanic*. Some people say it hit an iceberg because its owner, who was on board, forced the captain to sail too fast in dangerous waters. He wanted to break the speed record for crossing the Atlantic.

More than 700 people escaped the sinking ship in lifeboats.

The Carroll A. DEERING

Whatever happened to the *Carroll A. Deering* in 1921 must have happened fast. The crew had abandoned ship in a rush. In the kitchen, they had been preparing a meal. Both the lifeboats were gone, but none of the men on board were ever seen again.

Mystery words...

shoals: areas of shallow water where a ship may run aground

The schooner *Carroll A. Deering* was discovered in 1921. It had **run aground** on the Diamond Shoals, off the coast of North Carolina in the United States. But there was no sign of its 10-man crew—and no clues that might reveal why they had left the ship in such an unusual hurry.

Ships' Graveyard

Shipwrecks are common on the Diamond Shoals. Vessels run into rocks just below the ocean surface. Is that why the crew left in such a hurry? Were they attacked by pirates? Did a nearby hurricane play a part in the disaster? So far, there are still no clues.

There are many remote islands off the coast of North Carolina.

21

The Bermuda
TRIANGLE

The *Carroll A. Deering* may have been a victim of the Bermuda Triangle. This area is the most mysterious part of the oceans. For many decades, it has been the scene of unexplained disappearances.

The area lies between Florida, Bermuda, and Puerto Rico. It is said to have been the site of many losses over centuries. They include sailing ships and squadrons of U.S. warplanes from World War II, passenger planes, large merchant vessels, and small leisure yachts. The disappearances have no rational explanation. No trace of any wreckage has ever been found.

The Bermuda Triangle is the most mysterious body of water on Earth.

Range of Theories

People have come up with various **theories** about why so many ships vanish in the Bermuda Triangle. Some blame the losses on storms or sudden waves. Another theory is that magnetic forces disable navigation instruments, and lead ships to run aground. There are also more unusual suggestions. Some people claim the missing ships have been taken by aliens. But others reject the idea that the Bermuda Triangle is unusual. They say the disappearances are simply the kind of accidents that happen at sea.

Mystery File:
USS CYCLOPS

One of the biggest victims of the Bermuda Triangle was the USS *Cyclops*. It vanished without a trace in 1918. All 306 crewmen disappeared. The disaster was the single biggest noncombat loss of life in the history of the U.S. Navy.

Mystery words...

theories: unproved explanations for something

23

The Teignmouth ELECTRON

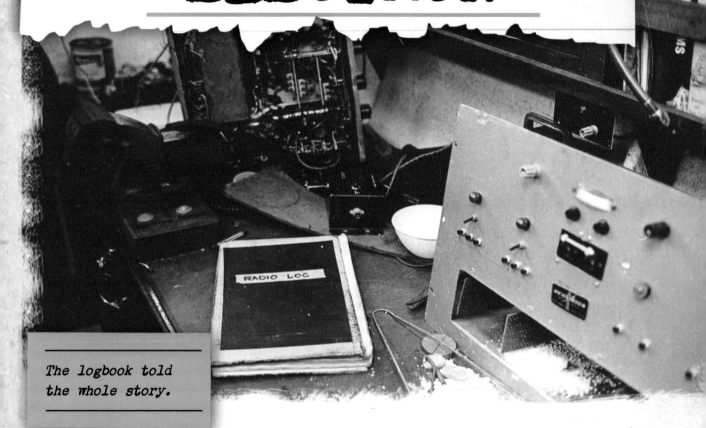

VOMECH

RADIO LOG

The trimaran drifting in the middle of the Atlantic Ocean in July 1969 was not supposed to be there. Everyone believed the Teignmouth Electron was taking part in an around-the-world race, somewhere in the southern oceans. Its skipper, Donald Crowhurst, had vanished.

Mystery words...

trimaran: a type of boat with three parallel hulls joined by a deck

Crowhurst had entered the race for solo sailors to try to win a cash prize. As he radioed in his position, it seemed that he was making good progress. He even held the lead. Then the *Teignmouth Electron* was found, empty and **adrift**.

A False Log

Crowhurst's logbook showed that the race had begun badly. He began to radio in false positions. He planned to stay in the Atlantic and then finish the race. But after about six months, the sailor may have jumped overboard to his death.

Mystery File: DEADLY STRESS

Evidence on the *Teignmouth Electron* suggests that Crowhurst may have gone crazy. He hoped to start a business with his prize money. Did loneliness and the stress of faking the records drive him mad enough to jump overboard?

Scared to DEATH

One day in 1948, ships near Indonesia picked up garbled **SOS** messages on the radio. A Dutch cargo ship, the *Ourang Medan*, was in distress—but the nature of the emergency was not clear. Nearby ships raced toward the Dutch vessel.

When they reached the *Ourang Medan*, it was too late. The crew were all dead. Even the ship's dog was dead. There was no sign of what had caused the deaths, but the rescuers were horrified to see that the men were frozen in poses of terror. They had been scared to death.

Did the merchant ship face some kind of supernatural horror?

Mysterious Explosion

The mystery of the dead crew needed further investigation. But almost at once, a fire broke out on the *Ourang Medan*, and the rescuers had to abandon ship. Before there was any chance to go back on board, there was a huge explosion. The ship sank, together with its crew.

What had become of the men? One theory is that something in the cargo had released gas that had poisoned the crew. The gas then built up in the cargo deck and caused the ship to explode.

Mystery File:
FATAL CHEMISTRY

Was the crew scared to death? If it is threatened, the body releases a chemical called adrenaline to fuel a getaway. But too much adrenaline can make the heart quiver. Could fear produce enough adrenaline to stop the heart?

Mystery words...

garbled: describing something difficult to hear or understand

27

Lost Ships of the
DESERT

In the late 19th century, ghost ships began to appear in the middle of the Colorado Desert in California.

The people who saw them could not believe their eyes. The wooden wrecks of abandoned sailing ships suddenly loomed up out of the dry desert; just as quickly, they were swallowed up again by the swirling sands.

Mystery words...

ferryboat: a boat that carries passengers on short voyages

Observers reported seeing two ancient Spanish sailing ships called galleons, a Viking ship with tall serpent necks at either end, and a **ferryboat**. They were miles from the nearest water, in the Gulf of California and the Colorado River.

Four Desert Ships

The vessels were probably real ships washed into the desert by giant waves or river floods. But we may never know. In 1905, a huge flood on the Colorado created the Salton Sea, leaving the desert and its ghost ships underwater.

Mystery File:
HIGH AND DRY

Many buried ships have been found far from water. In 1998, construction workers in Pisa, Italy, unearthed the wrecks of 16 ancient cargo ships. When they sank, in A.D. 200, the area had been a port. The coastline had moved over time.

The ghost ships now lie beneath the waters of the Salton Sea.

29

Glossary

adrift Floating without power

cargo A load transported between locations in return for payment

ferryboat A boat that carries passengers on short voyages

flares Bright lights fired into the sky as distress signals

garbled Describes something difficult to hear or understand

log The official record of a ship's voyage

man-of-war A heavily armed warship with sails

merchant ship A ship used to carry cargo for trade

mutiny An uprising by sailors or soldiers against their officers or captain

navigate To work out and follow a course of direction

paddle wheel A wheel driven by a motor to move a boat

phenomena Things that are not easily explained

run aground For a ship to crash into rocks or land and become stuck

schooner A sailboat with two or more masts, used for carrying cargo

shoals Areas of shallow water where a ship may run aground

SOS The radio code used to call for help in an emergency

superstition A belief that events can magically create bad luck

theories Unproved explanations for something

trimaran A type of boat with three parallel hulls joined by a deck

Find Out More

BOOKS

Hamilton, Sue L. *Air and Sea Mysteries* (Unsolved Mysteries). ABDO and Daughters, 2007.

Konstam, Angus. *Ghost Ships: Tales of Abandoned, Doomed, and Haunted Vessels*. Lyons Press, 2007.

Korman, Gordon. *Titanic: SOS*. Scholastic Paperbacks, 2011.

Stone, Adam. *The Bermuda Triangle* (Torque Books: The Unexplained). Bellwether Media, 2010.

Yolen, Jane, and Heidi Stemple. *The Mary Celeste: An Unsolved Mystery from History.* Simon and Schuster, 2009.

WEBSITES

List of ghost ships
Listverse Top 10 ghost ships from history.
http://listverse.com/2011/01/02/top-10-ghost-ships/

Ghost ships described
Museum of Unnatural Mystery
http://www.unmuseum.org/phantomship.htm

Bermuda Triangle
How Stuff Works explanation of the Bermuda Triangle
http://adventure.howstuffworks.com/bermuda-triangle.htm

Titanic mystery
Encyclopedia of the *Titanic* sinking, including the "mystery ship"
www.encyclopedia-titanica.org

Index